OLYMPIC
NATIONAL PARK
& THE OLYMPIC
PENINSULA

A TRAVELER'S COMPANION

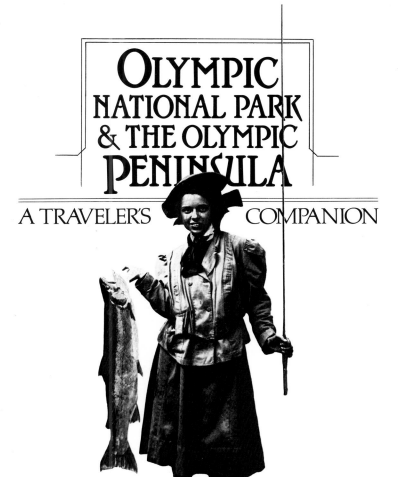

By Robert Steelquist

Photography by Pat O'Hara, Cindy McIntyre, and Keith D. Lazelle, Designed by McQuiston & Daughter
Published by Woodlands Press in conjunction with Pacific Northwest National Parks and Forests Association

GRAYWOLF RIVER

CONTENTS

THE RUGGED COASTAL WILDERNESS OF OLYMPIC NATIONAL PARK

ABOUT THIS BOOK

The Olympic Peninsula comprises nearly 6,400 square miles of land—mountains, valleys, and coastal shores—tacked onto the northwestern corner of Washington State. Although the heart and soul of this rugged landscape is wilderness, it is circled by U.S. Highway 101, giving motorists more than just a glimpse of its great variety of scenery and affording ample opportunity to participate in a wide range of recreational activities.

This book is designed to get you around the peninsula and into its midst, where you can sample and enjoy the landforms and natural environments as well as the communities and lifestyles that make up this small corner of the United States.

The book is divided into three sections that correspond to the major geographic regions that surround the Olympic Mountains: "Rain Country" (the western coastal strip); "The Fabled Strait" (the foothills to the north along the Strait of Juan de Fuca); and "Steep Rivers" (the narrow ribbon of lowland along Hood Canal, to the east). Each chapter begins with a brief historical narrative about the early exploration of the particular region and then describes the major attractions found there. Also included are information on campgrounds and services necessary to the visitor, as well as maps showing routes and destinations.

The book is intended to help you plan your trip to the peninsula so that the only surprises you will encounter are the ones you seek—the sight of an elk herd, a gorgeous sunset, a moss-draped rain forest maple. It is a book that I hope you will find useful before, during, and after your visit to the Olympic Peninsula.

OLYMPIC NATIONAL PARK
(U.S. DEPARTMENT OF INTERIOR)

Olympic National Park was established in 1938 in order to protect, for future generations, a large tract of the wild Olympic Peninsula. It is managed in such a manner as to preserve the landscape, with its living resources and natural processes, as it appeared at the time of European settlement. Regulations prohibit hunting, possession of firearms, offroad vehicle use, and the disturbance of plants and wildlife. Fishing is permitted in accordance with state regulations. For further information about National Park Service policies, write to: Superintendent, Olympic National Park, 600 East Park Avenue, Port Angeles, Washington 98362.

OLYMPIC NATIONAL FOREST
(U.S. DEPARTMENT OF AGRICULTURE)

Olympic National Forest was established to manage renewable resources such as timber, water, forage, and wildlife under the principles of multiple use and sustained yield. Portions of Olympic National Forest are managed as wilderness—motorized vehicles are not permitted there. Throughout the forest however, hunting and fishing are permitted according to state regulations, and collection of firewood and live plants is allowed with a permit. For more information regarding U.S. Forest Service policies, write to: Forest Supervisor, Olympic National Forest, 801 S. Capitol Way, P. O. Box 2288, Olympia, Washington 98507.

MT. OLYMPUS

INTRODUCTION

The trail was rough and circuitous, over hills, gulches and canyons. Great trees lay across it so that for pack animals it was impassable and even for a man it was little better than no trail at all."—From the diary of Charles Barnes of the Press Expedition, 1890. The Olympic Peninsula has always been a challenge to travelers. It was not until well into this century that overland travel was even possible without the kind of hardship described by Charles Barnes.

It has always been an unruly land, furrowed by deep river valleys, barricaded by alpine obstructions, cloaked in a tangle of forests and bogs—a system of impasses, designed, it would seem, to frustrate the hurrying traveler.

Visible from a great distance from both sea and land, the Olympics form a bold massif of forested slopes, ragged peaks, and mysterious river valleys. The eye is drawn along the sawblade of summits, through the blue-green foothills, and down the ochre bluffs that extend to water boundaries. Colors are muted, softened by occasional cloud cover and mists. Cool pigments lie easily on the eye. Successions of shapes seem outlined by airbrush shadows, highlighted by the glisten of slanted light.

Into this compelling environment, human presence has advanced only slowly. Patterns of settlement follow the patterns of the shore and river valleys, reminding us that getting around *on* the peninsula has long been—and remains—a matter of getting *around* the peninsula. Roads have not been constructed through the heart of the mountains to preserve the wilderness. To cross directly from Hood Canal on the east to the Pacific requires time and physical stamina, as mountain passes can be crossed only on footpaths. But it is possible to get a sense of the Olympic Peninsula, its scenery and its life forms, by circling it via highway and making side trips along slender roads that lead to forest, meadow, and shore.

The time needed for a full experiencing of the Olympic Peninsula varies from visitor to visitor. Simply stated, the more time, the better. But a few moments can hold as many surprises as a few days, if you are in the right place and frame of mind. Your trip may be made memorable by a glimpse of a golden eagle soaring quickly in and out of sight at Hurricane Ridge, a herd of Roosevelt elk secretively crossing the Hoh Road, or a coho salmon thrashing over the cascades along the Soleduck River. Moments are what stand out in any recollection of a place visited—the instant when the light changed, a wind arose, or a sudden vista connected disembodied localities and the whole world seemed visible and true. Time is therefore not as important as one's perspective. The ready visitor can sense it all in moments.

Nevertheless, getting around the 310-mile circumference of the peninsula with enough time to taste each of its major natural components requires two or three days. To get a sense of the communities of people, to learn of their past and to celebrate their present, requires more time. A week spent ambling on the Olympic Peninsula will leave the visitor with a collage of impressions—as well as with the satisfaction of not having passed through too quickly.

THE LAND

About 35 to 50 million years ago, what we now call the Olympic Range was being formed on the bottom of the Pacific Ocean.

At that time, waves lapped at the continental edge somewhere to the east of present-day Seattle—no peninsula or island arose out of the water where the Olympics now stand. The formation of this range was poorly understood until geologists accepted the theory that the earth's surface is composed of great plates of moving crust that float on a liquid mantle. Where these plates collide, vast sections of the earth's surface are often welded together. When a plate of oceanic crust contacts a plate of continental crust, the oceanic crust usually slips beneath the edge of the continent. Current theory suggests that the Olympics represent sedimentary deposits that settled on the oceanic crust and volcanic lava that rose through fissures in the crust. As the oceanic crust slid beneath the continent, the rocks that now form the Olympics were skimmed off and added to the continental edge.

Basalt, the hard black rock formed from lava, is found in a horseshoe-shaped formation along the north, east, and southeast perimeter of the peninsula. Deformed sandstones and shales that formed from sediments make up the inner Olympic peaks, including Mount Olympus. The material that was forced under the continent melted and is responsible for the volcanic activity that formed the Cascades.

Once this mass of seafloor material had become attached to the continent, the process of erosion took over, whittling, gouging, and polishing the mountains to

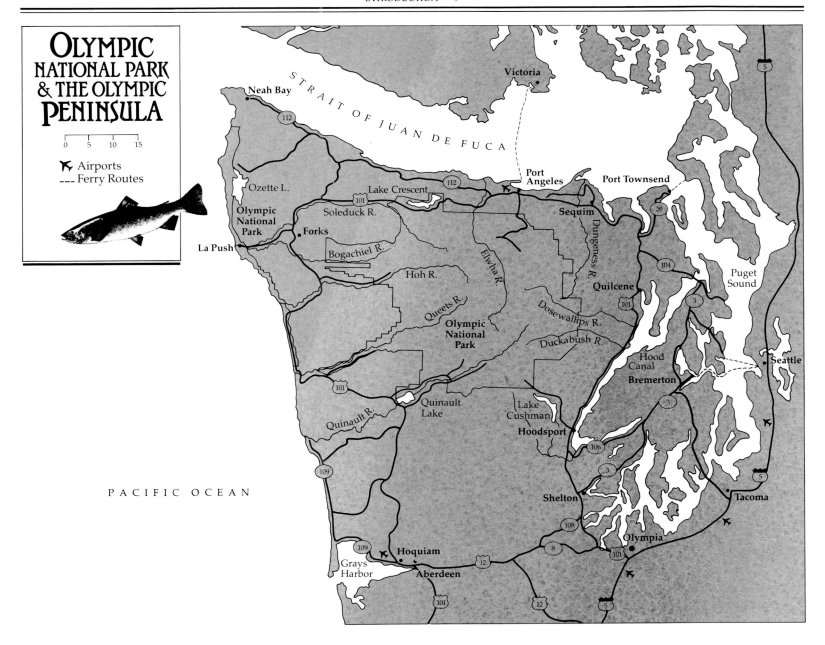

OLYMPIC NATIONAL PARK & THE OLYMPIC PENINSULA

0 5 10 15

✈ Airports
--- Ferry Routes

STRAIT OF JUAN DE FUCA

PACIFIC OCEAN

Neah Bay

Victoria

Port Angeles

Port Townsend

Ozette L.

Lake Crescent

Olympic National Park

Soleduck R.

Sequim

Dungeness R.

Forks

Bogachiel R.

La Push

Hoh R.

Elwha R.

Quilcene

Puget Sound

Queets R.

Olympic National Park

Dosewallips R.

Duckabush R.

Hood Canal

Bremerton

Seattle

Quinault R.

Quinault Lake

Lake Cushman

Hoodsport

Shelton

Tacoma

Hoquiam

Olympia

Grays Harbor

Aberdeen

112

101

104

20

101

3

106

3

108

8

101

109

109

12

101

12

5

5

3

produce the intensely sculpted Olympic Range that we see today. Water—in both liquid form and glacial ice—continues the sculpting process, in seasonal cycles of freshet (flooding) and the much slower process of glacial advance and retreat.

The more than sixty active glaciers in Olympic National Park give present tense to geologic time. The fact that the Olympics hold some of the world's most accessible glaciers has added greatly to our scientific knowledge and aesthetic appreciation of these spectacular natural landforms.

THE CLIMATE

Standing apart from the other mountain ranges of the Pacific Northwest, the Olympics create their own climate. Latitude and the maritime setting favor the region with moderate temperatures year-round. Nevertheless, summer days and nights can be chilly, especially at higher elevations. Summer coastal fogs are common. A sweater and a water-repellent windbreaker are advisable. Spring and fall clothing should be on the warm side, with wool and synthetic fillers and fibers preferable to down because of the dampness. Well-sealed footwear is recommended all year because of water and mud on trails. One should dress for the worst in winter. Hurricane Ridge, which is accessible most of the winter, lives up to its name with icy winds as well as many feet of snowfall. Lowlands don't receive much snow in winter, but they make up for it with rain.

The Olympic Mountains block the moist maritime air masses blowing in from the Pacific, forcing the damp air to rise. As it climbs the western flanks of the range, the air cools rapidly and its moisture tumbles out in the form of rain (and, at higher elevations during winter, as snow). As the air continues to rise over the mountains it becomes successively drier. By the time it reaches the northeast side of the mountains—known locally as the "rain shadow"—scant moisture remains, and less rain falls. As a result, the Olympic Peninsula can boast both the wettest and driest areas of the coastal Pacific Northwest.

To the visitor, the difference between the "wet" and "dry" sides of the Olympics is not particularly apparent, since both areas receive rainfall at any time during the year and both have extended periods of dryness. Weather on either side of the mountains is difficult to predict. The same raincoat you bring along for the trip to the coast could prove just as handy when you go through Sequim ("skwim"), in the heart of "the rain shadow."

PLANTS AND ANIMALS

Several isolating mechanisms have played important roles in shaping the plant and animal communities of the Olympics. The physical separation of the peninsula from other nearby mountain ranges has left the Olympic high country an island in a biological sense. Animals, such as the Olympic chipmunk and the Olympic marmot, and plants, such as Flett's violet and Piper's bellflower, have been isolated for the millennia necessary to evolve independently of their Cascade Range and Vancouver Island relatives.

Similarly, the moat that surrounds the Olympics—consisting of lowlands, seawater, and, at times, glacial ice—has prevented many animals and plants from ever becoming established here. Among animals found in neighboring regions but not in the Olympics are the porcupine, badger, bighorn sheep, and grizzly bear.

Animals that have established large populations on the peninsula include Roosevelt elk, black bears, cougars, bobcats, black tailed deer, and a host of other mammals. One major predator—the timber wolf—was eliminated from the Olympic ecosystem in the 1920s. Elk are quite common in the rain forest valleys of the west side of the peninsula. Research conducted in Olympic National Park has found that, contrary to earlier belief, not all elk herds migrate between high meadows and lowland valleys. Some herds actually remain in the lowland forest year-round, affording summer visitors a chance to see the majestic mammals as they move among the moss-draped trees of the rain forest.

Deer, black bears, and Olympic marmots are common at Hurricane Ridge. Summer explosions of wildflowers, particularly American bistort, provide nourishing forage for black tailed deer. Black bears are seen moving along distant slopes, pawing decaying logs and foraging among meadow shrubs. Marmots, the largest members of the squirrel family, sun themselves on the heaps of "mine tailings" that serve as the porches of their subterranean dens.

Continued on page 14

ROOSEVELT ELK (*CERVIS CANADENSIS*) were the main reason that President
Theodore Roosevelt established Mt. Olympus National Monument in 1909.
The world's largest unmanaged population of these stately animals thrives
on the peninsula as a living memorial to the great conservationist.

FISHING ON THE PENINSULA

In a region where the sound of moving water is nearly everywhere, the ecological, recreational, and economic roles of fish cannot be overlooked. Sportfishing has always attracted visitors to the peninsula and remains a popular activity.

Pacific salmon are well represented by five species: Chinook, or "king," salmon; coho, or "silver," salmon; pink, or "humpbacked," salmon; sockeye, or "red," salmon; and chum, or "dog," salmon. Each year, usually in the fall, runs of each of these species return to the streams of their origin. Salmon stocks are managed cooperatively by Indian tribes, state agencies, and federal agencies, and public interest and support for the maintenance of wild stocks remains high. Charterboat fishing for salmon is available in nearly every port—check local yellow-page listings for operators.

Sea-running forms of rainbow and cutthroat trout are also prevalent. "Steelhead," the ocean-going rainbow trout, attracts fishermen from all over the world. In fact, for many anglers the names Hoh, Bogachiel, and Soleduck are synonymous with "steelhead." Winter runs of steelhead are larger than summer runs, but summer fish are taken. Cutthroat trout can be caught along saltwater beaches throughout the summer.

"Resident" trout—rainbow, cutthroat, and Dolly Varden and Eastern brook (both of which are actually char, not trout)—that do not leave fresh water are found in streams and lakes throughout the Olympics.

Fishing in Olympic National Park is permitted without a state license; punchcards for steelhead and salmon are required, however. Certain park waters are subject to special regulations, so it is best to check at the nearest ranger station before fishing.

Fishing on reservation waters by non-Indians is regulated by tribes and is subject to tribal license. Elsewhere on the peninsula, a state license is necessary for anyone over the age of sixteen. Many sporting goods outlets carry regulations brochures. Particular attention should be paid to special local restrictions and closures.

OLYMPIC RIVERS host runs of five species of Pacific salmon. (*Above*) A gleaming coho or silver salmon. At right, an early Olympic recreationist holds a steelhead trout taken in the upper waters of the Elwha River, where dam construction eliminated these fish in 1911. (*Opposite*) Chris Morgenroth, the first district ranger employed to oversee Mt. Olympus National Monument (before the creation of Olympic National Park), tries to coax another trout "from fishin' hole to fryin' pan."

While this isolation has limited, to some degree, the types of plants and animals found on the peninsula, it has contributed greatly to the diversity of living things that we can see and appreciate close at hand.

Every February and March, California gray whales migrate northward along the Olympic shore, en route to feeding grounds in the Bering Sea. In December and January, pregnant females are seen heading south to the calving lagoons off the Baja Peninsula in Mexico. Migratory shorebirds and waterfowl pass in multitudes, pausing at places like Bowerman Basin, on the northern shore of Grays Harbor, and Dungeness Spit, on the Strait of Juan de Fuca.

Salmon move along the nutrient-rich continental shelf, some bound for Olympic rivers, others heading toward rivers and streams that drain the maritime slopes of the Alaska, British Columbia, Oregon, and California coasts.

The presence of four life zones (elevation layers with characteristic plants and animals) gives the Olympic Peninsula a magnificent variety of flora and fauna, a textbook example of the way living things arrange themselves according to the conditions under which they must survive.

The climatic variation between east and west is vividly displayed in the plant com-

THE SETTLEMENT OF the Olympic Peninsula meant optimism and industry to newcomers—rich valley soils promised heavy crops, and the forests promised wealth. To the Indians, it meant transformation—old ways lost, new ways adopted.

munities of the Olympic Range. The wet west side hosts communities at peace with the gloomy dampness that accompanies the up to 160 inches of annual rainfall. Similarly, the seasonally arid regions of the northeastern Olympics display plant types more at home in hotter climates, such as the brittle cactus and Garry oak of the Sequim prairie, where rainfall averages about 16 inches per year.

The most notable climate-dependent plant community found here is the temperate rain forest—one of the most spectacular forest types of the northern hemisphere. Best seen in the river valleys of the Hoh, the Queets, and the Quinault, the rain forest is an explosion of arboreal extravagance. A profusion of clubmoss, ferns, and liverworts thrive on the nourishment of rain water and air as they adorn the trunks and limbs of maples, alder, fir, hemlock, and spruce.

Elsewhere around the peninsula, the lowland forest and its dense undergrowth form a lush tangle. Western hemlock and western redcedar thrive in the soft light of the forest. A thick mantle of dead needles covers the ground, forming a rich acidic humus. Shy forest flowers, such as trillium and Calypso orchid, are found deep in the forest shade.

The middle-elevation forests are often dominated by Pacific silver fir in the moist western portions of Olympic National Park and by western hemlock and Douglas-fir in the drier northeastern region. Windstorm and wildfire are the two factors most important to the maintenance of Douglas-fir in the natural forest. In the managed forests outside Olympic National Park, Douglas-fir owes its prevalence to replanting, because of its value as a timber tree.

Mountain country means superb scenery—and unique subalpine plant life. Parklike meadows burst into bloom during the short-lived days of summer with showy displays of lupine and avalanche lilies. Stunted trees recall winter burdens of deep-lying snow and dehydrating icy winds. The spirelike forms of subalpine firs—shaped to shed snow—remind us that even in a mild region, elevation can contribute to extremity.

THE PEOPLE

Settlement on the Olympic Peninsula has always been centered around water, fringing coves, harbors, and the junctions of rivers. The First Americans—the Quinault, Hoh, Quileute, Makah, Klallam, Chimacum, and Skokomish—established permanent winter villages around the perimeter of the peninsula. Summer camps for elk and deer hunting were scattered around the edges of the high country, while fishing camps were located at remote beaches and spits or at the mouths of creeks.

Not surprisingly, European settlers chose town sites and harbors for the same reasons as their native predecessors: water access and shelter from wind and wave. The first European settlement on the peninsula was the Spanish outpost of Nuñez Gaona, established in 1792 near the Makah village at Neah Bay. The founding of this settlement marked the final act of expansion for the Spanish Empire. Upon the settlement's abandonment the following year, the Spanish grip over the Pacific Northwest loosened.

Westward expansion of the American nation brought settlers to the Olympic shores only after the majority of land elsewhere in the Puget Sound region had been claimed. They founded towns near deep-water moorages so that supplies from Seattle and Victoria could be within easy reach. Towns vied for the hoped-for railroad terminus, and some fell hard when the dream evaporated.

Port Angeles got its start as a federal land reserve, set aside by President Abraham Lincoln for its harbor, military base, lighthouse, and customs station. Enterprising settlers "jumped" the government claim, however, and the town site was opened to the squatters by proclamation of President Grover Cleveland in 1891.

Olympic Peninsula timber made kings of many men in the heydays of ox and horse, then steam, and finally diesel. Farming in the Dungeness Valley, where irrigation overcame the arid prairie, produced bumper crops of oats, barley, wheat, and peas. "Stump farms" sprang up all around the peninsula—marginal operations where vegetables and dairy products were produced as subsistence and cash crops. Often a small sawmill out back provided additional income. Canneries packed clams and salmon for markets as distant as San Francisco.

Once word got around that the Olympics were a recreational paradise, resorts began dotting the shores of lakes and streams and developing near hot springs and beaches. With the completion in 1931 of the Olympic Peninsula loop highway, the tourism boom commenced in earnest.

The establishment of Olympic National Park in 1938 put the peninsula on the map for the entire nation. Carved out of the central portion of the mountain range and extending down several of the major rivers and along a portion of the Pacific coast, Olympic National Park remains the major attraction for visitors to the peninsula.

Timber and fishing continue to provide the livelihood for many peninsula residents, but the focus is shifting. The end of the old-growth timber resource and competition from other timber-producing regions have forced the timber industry to shift gears, emphasizing leaner harvest operations and more intensive regeneration programs. Similarly, salmon stocks hover at greatly reduced numbers, and quota restrictions have forced many commercial fishermen to seek work "on the beach."

Nevertheless, towns of the Olympic Peninsula boast diversified industries, varied commercial services, excellent tourism facilities, numerous cultural events and festivals, and, of course, year-round recreational opportunities found in few other places. A unique heritage of life at the edge of the continent and a genuine appreciation of the peninsula's resources make the local folks the peninsula's biggest fans. Whether you go picking blackberries, oysters, or wild mushrooms or hiking on the beaches or mountain trails, the people you encounter are just as likely to be residents as visitors.

THE BILL OF CONGRESS that established the Oregon Territory also authorized several light-houses for the newly acquired west coast. Cape Flattery was one of nine locations selected, and the lighthouse, built in 1857, led shippers safely into the Strait of Juan de Fuca. The lighthouse used a Fresnel (*fra-nel*) lens, shown below, developed by a French physicist in 1822. The concentric prisms of the lens concentrated the light, magnifying it thousands of times.

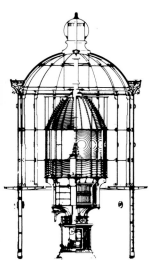

SOLEDUCK FALLS

THE WESTERN SIDE

RAIN COUNTRY

The Hoh River was swollen from rain and the color of an old nickel. Winter rainshowers had brought the water up, and it had been chewing away the gray clay banks upriver. Rainwater continued to drip from the bare tree limbs that hung over the river, although the rain itself had stopped falling a half-hour before. The outboard motor whined and the skiff in which I was a passenger cut downstream over the opaque surface of the river.

e approached the river's mouth, where the blue-gray Pacific crashed against the bar in rollers that, from low on the river, looked at least two stories high. We passed the last buildings of the old Hoh village and swung along the steep cobbled beach that lines the widened river mouth. I twisted around in my seat in the bow to look at the breakers. They drew themselves up the beach and collapsed in bursts of brilliant white. The roar was deafening.

We approached the thin strand that separates the relatively calm water of the river from the chaos of the beach. Here the bar narrows and disappears beneath a point where fresh and salt water begin to blend. The gray of the ocean matched the gray of the sky, which itself borrowed the gray of the river. In this choppy netherworld of water, the cycle of sea, air, mountain, and river completes itself daily. The land, reduced to particles suspended in the river, slips into the ocean, where it will settle and, in millions of years, rise again. Seawater, evaporated into a thick overcast, flies inland, where it will fall as rain.

I was a little relieved when, within feet of the threatening surf, my host swung the boat back upriver. Wedged in the tight vee of the bow and gazing astern, I now faced the ocean. Breakers hovered over the shoulders of the Hoh fisherman like a blanket, a cape. The backdrop churned with energy. Slowly, the drone of the outboard again became audible over the roar of the waves. A glint of sunlight reflected off the slickened shoulders of my companion's raincoat—it had started raining again. The skiff planed upriver, over the nickel-colored water.

I am not the first person to have felt, close at hand, the awesome converging powers of river, rain, and sea along the Olympic coast. Many have not enjoyed this sensation, for this wild coast has taken a heavy toll of ships—and lives.

The earliest recorded shipwreck here was that of the Russian brig *St. Nicholas*, in 1808. While exploring the coast near the mouth of the Hoh River, the vessel foundered and spent a long night being tossed in the current among dangerous rocks that pricked the surface of the near-shore water. Just south of the Quillayute River, the vessel at last rested, her hull pierced by the teeth of the rocky coast. All aboard reached the shore safely and began a bizarre odyssey along the shore, hoping to make Grays Harbor, nearly 70 miles to the south.

The band attempted to move undetected by the local natives, aware that two other landing parties had been killed in the vicinity decades earlier. Contact was inevitable, however, and when the group reached the mouth of the Hoh, they tensely negotiated the assistance of the Hoh people, who provided canoes and paddlers for the crossing. But in the middle of the river, the natives swamped and abandoned the canoes. The party was divided and several members were captured, including the captain's fair-haired wife, who became a prized slave. Those remaining free regrouped, heading upriver to avoid capture. They managed to elude the Indians for nearly a year, living in the forest of the Hoh Valley. Eventually, part of the group elected to surrender. The others constructed a boat and attempted a daring escape downriver. While they were crossing the bar of the Hoh River, the boat was upset, and they, too, were made captives. The Russians were traded to several neighboring tribes, including the Makah. The captain's wife became the property of an illustrious Makah chief and enjoyed, for a time, a degree of prestige and luxury. She was traded away, however, to a chief of less noble qualities, and at length she became despondent and took her own life, or so the story goes. Other crew members survived among the Indians and were eventually ransomed to an American sea captain. After nearly two years ashore on the Olympic Peninsula, thirteen of the original twenty crewmen were returned to Sitka to tell their harrowing tales of the rain country.

The coastal side of the Olympic Peninsula is a moody place, balanced between the vacant Pacific horizon and the confusing array of peaks and valleys of the mountain range. Towns are spaced widely, connected by long stretches of highway

THE WESTERN SIDE
RAIN COUNTRY

0	5	10	15

◆ Information Centers
◇ Seasonal Information
   Centers
△ Campgrounds
▲ State Parks
--- Ferry Routes

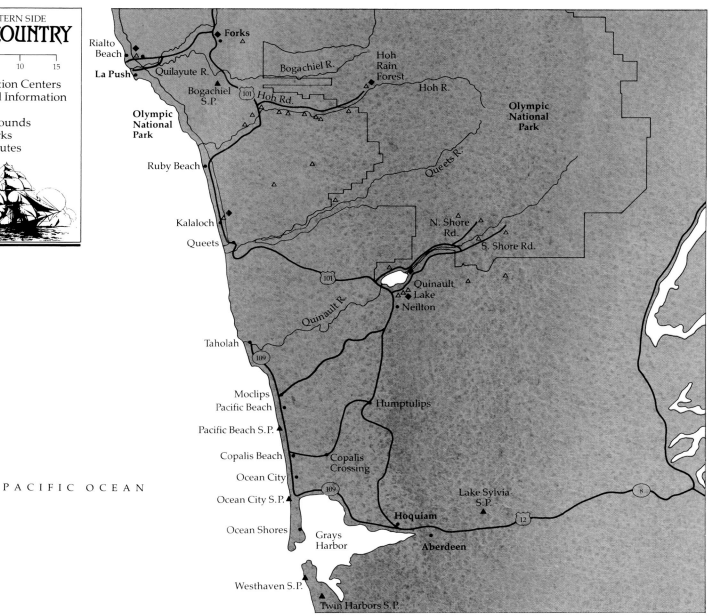

Forks

Rialto
Beach

La Push

Quilayute R.

Bogachiel R.

Hoh
Rain
Forest

Hoh R.

101

Hoh Rd.

Bogachiel
S.P.

Olympic
National
Park

Olympic
National
Park

Ruby Beach

Queets R.

Kalaloch

N. Shore
Rd.

Queets

S. Shore Rd.

101

Quinault
Lake
Neilton

Quinault R.

Taholah

109

Moclips
Pacific Beach

Humptulips

Pacific Beach S.P.

Copalis Beach

Copalis
Crossing

Ocean City

Lake Sylvia
S.P.

PACIFIC OCEAN

Ocean City S.P.

109

8

Ocean Shores

12

Hoquiam

Grays
Harbor

Aberdeen

Westhaven S.P.

Twin Harbors S.P.

SINCE ITS ESTABLISHMENT, Hoquiam has been a commercial link between dark Olympic forests and timber markets of the world. The rowdy histories of logging and seafaring converged here, leaving a colorful heritage. This view shows the town, on the banks of the Hoquiam River, as it appeared in 1888. (*Opposite*) Sunrise at Toleak Point, on the South Coast Wilderness of Olympic National Park.

that alternately border towering forests and clearcut spaces. Peppered along the roadside are small shake and shingle mills, some active, some idle. Cafes and gas stations are sparse, and motels and resorts are generally clustered in or near the towns.

The coast itself varies in accessibility and in topography. The southern beaches are just a short walk from the road shoulder and are broad and sandy. The northern beaches, particularly within the ocean strip of Olympic National Park, are more remote and rugged. Inland, the river valleys differ in the condition of their roads and in the distance they penetrate into the mountains. The only fully paved westside road inland into Olympic National Park is the Hoh Road, leading to the Hoh Rain Forest. Opportunities for recreation are varied. Campgrounds, trails, and picnic areas are sprinkled along both sides of U.S. 101. Clam digging attracts many visitors to the southern beaches, while winter steelhead fishing attracts many to the rivers.

Throughout the year, the coastal area is a wildlife watcher's paradise. California gray whales spout close to shore on their winter and spring migrations. Tidepool life teems in the rocky clefts, while seabirds clutter the offshore rocks. Eagles pick over salmon carcasses along the rivers and beaches, and elk browse together in forest openings.

GRAYS HARBOR

Grays Harbor is named for Captain Robert Gray, who crossed the bar at its entrance in 1792. Since then it has grown in importance as a seaport. The harbor's twin cities of Aberdeen and Hoquiam each support

active commerce in wood pulp, lumber, and shipping.

Aberdeen is located at the head of the harbor, along the estuary formed by the Chehalis River. State Route 12 links it to Olympia, 48 miles east. Motels, gas stations, garages, restaurants, grocery stores, and other services are available here.

Neighboring Hoquiam borders to the west. Here the motorist can choose between U.S. 101, which leads north toward Lake Quinault, or State Route 109, which continues along the north shore of Grays Harbor toward Ocean Shores, Copalis, Moclips, and Taholah.

Hoquiam features several sights of interest, including the Polson Logging Museum and the Hoquiam Castle, former residence of a local timber baron. Meals, lodging, groceries, gas, auto repair, fishing tackle, and outdoor supplies are available. Bowerman Basin, with its vast springtime flocks of migratory shorebirds and accompanying peregrine falcons, is west of Hoquiam along State Route 109.

SOUTH OLYMPIC BEACHES
Ocean Shores sits on a peninsula that juts into the entrance of Grays Harbor from the north. This fast-growing commercial resort area offers motels, a convention center, restaurants, motorbike rentals, and a public golf course. Development is concentrated around Ocean Shores and begins to taper off north of Ocean City. From there north to Moclips, resorts are mostly clustered in the towns of Copalis Beach, Pacific Beach, and Moclips. Until recently, the area attracted throngs of clam diggers to its wide, sandy beaches. However, in the last few years the razor clams have suffered devastating parasite attacks, believed by some to have been aggravated by the 1982 El Niño warm-water phenomenon. Clamming will resume once the stocks have recovered.

Several state parks are located in the area. Ocean City State Park, just south of Ocean City, has 179 campsites and 29 trailer hookups. Pacific Beach State Park, 13 miles north of Ocean City, has 105 campsites and 10 trailer hookups. The broad beach can be reached from numerous public access points dotted along the road.

At Moclips, State Route 109 is met by a Quinault tribal road that connects to U.S.

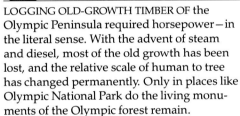

LOGGING OLD-GROWTH TIMBER OF the Olympic Peninsula required horsepower—in the literal sense. With the advent of steam and diesel, most of the old growth has been lost, and the relative scale of human to tree has changed permanently. Only in places like Olympic National Park do the living monuments of the Olympic forest remain.

101, 21 miles to the east. Most of this road is unpaved. State Route 109 continues north, crossing into the Quinault Indian Reservation. Some of the most picturesque coastline of the whole south coast is found along this section of the road, but access to the beach is limited to tribe members. At Taholah, the business center for the Quinault Nation, the road ends—for the time being. Negotiations between the Quinault tribe and Washington State have opened the way for the construction of a highway link that will border the coastline to the Queets River, where U.S. 101 approaches the coast from inland.

HUMPTULIPS AND NEILTON

Motorists who want to forgo the trip along the developed south Olympic coast can follow U.S. 101 from Hoquiam north toward Humptulips, Neilton, and Quinault. The highway clings to the bank of the west fork of the Hoquiam River, past rafted logs awaiting the float downstream to the mills or loading docks of Grays Harbor. At Humptulips, 22 miles north of Hoquiam, U.S. 101 is joined by a connecting link to the coast that passes through Copalis Crossing.

QUINAULT LAKE

At Quinault Lake, the motorist can choose to continue along U.S. 101 or to take either of the two routes uplake and along the two tributary forks of the Quinault River. The South Shore Road leads into the town of Quinault and to Olympic National Forest recreation areas, while the North Shore Road goes into Olympic National Park. The roads eventually meet upvalley and lead to spectacular rain forest groves. Only the lower portion of either road is paved, and neither is suitable for longer trailers or

KALALOCH LODGE ITSELF IS QUITE SPECIAL, but its location makes it more so. Set on the ocean within the Olympic National Park boundaries, the lodge and its outlying cabins are graced with shoreline beauty—meadows, estuaries, forest, and wide, uncrowded beaches. The western stretch of the park is the largest coastal wilderness in the contiguous United States; Kalaloch lies in the southernmost tip, close to the Queets River and just a short drive to the Queets and Quinault rain forests.

RVs. Occasionally, both roads suffer from washouts, so inquire at local ranger stations about road conditions. Because Quinault Lake is within the Quinault Indian Reservation, use of the lake is regulated by the tribe. Check locally for fishing and boating regulations.

The South Shore Road is paved in its lower stretches near the lake but turns to gravel as it enters the narrow belt of farmland beyond the lake. The town of Quinault is about 2½ miles off U.S. 101. Groceries and gas are available, as are overnight lodging and restaurant facilities. The Quinault Ranger District (U.S. Forest Service) headquarters is located in the middle of town. Information can be obtained there regarding Forest Service campsites, picnic areas, and trails into the Colonel Bob Wilderness Area, established in 1984. Falls Creek and Willaby campgrounds are both nearby. Gatton Creek Picnic Area is a short distance farther.

The South Shore Road continues beyond the lake, winding up the river valley. At about 12 miles, it enters Olympic National Park. A mile beyond the park boundary, it passes a bridge that connects it to the North Shore Road. The South Shore Road continues through the rain forest lowland to Graves Creek Ranger Station (staffed only in summer) and Campground, 18½ miles from U.S. 101. Less than a mile farther, the road ends and the trails to Enchanted Valley and Graves Creek begin. Enchanted Valley is known for its steep, towering walls and numerous waterfalls. It was one of the favorite hiking areas of the late Supreme Court Justice William O. Douglas.

The North Shore Road leaves U.S. 101 about 3 miles beyond the South Shore Road and enters the park almost immediately. It is paved for the first 12½ miles. July Creek Campground (National Park Service) is 3 miles off U.S. 101. Fewer services are available on the north side of the lake than on the south side, but some lodging is available. The Quinault Ranger Station (National Park Service) is 6 miles up the North Shore Road. Stop here for back-country and campground information. About 15 miles up the valley, the road passes some old homestead sites and the bridge that connects it to the South Shore Road. Continuing up the North Fork Quinault Road, you reach North Fork Campground and Ranger Station (staffed only in summer) and trailhead, approximately 18 miles from U.S. 101.

QUEETS

North of Lake Quinault, U.S. 101 heads toward the coast. About 20 miles from the lake, the Queets Road leads inland. The Queets Corridor is a thin strip of Olympic National Park added by President Harry Truman in 1953. It contains spectacular examples of rain forest and lowland river valley ecosystems. The Queets sideroad is unpaved for all of its 14-mile length and is not suitable for large trailers or RVs. The Queets Ranger Station, staffed only in the summer, is 12½ miles from U.S. 101. Queets Campground and a 3-mile nature loop trail are located a mile beyond the station. Hikers should be aware that the

Queets River trail begins on the *opposite* side of the river from the parking area; wading is necessary—and hazardous—much of the year.

KALALOCH

North of the village of Queets, Highway 101 breaks into a straight stretch just above the beach. This is the southernmost tip of the coastal strip of Olympic National Park. Kalaloch ("kuh-lay-lock") is about 3 miles north of the boundary. It features a picturesque lodge and restaurant, gas station, grocery store, campground, and ranger station. The ranger station, on the east side of the highway, has maps, books, tide tables, and other information.

WATER IS A SYMBOL OF LIFE. Olympic streams, born in glaciers and lush meadows, feed rivers that run to the sea, signifying the perpetual cycle that connects land to ocean — amid the network of living things.

Kalaloch Campground is the most popular in the park and fills to capacity every weekend and nearly every night during the summer season. A nature trail is close by, and park naturalists conduct campfire programs and tidepool walks between July 1 and Labor Day.

Numerous beach trails lead off U.S. 101; well-marked trailheads with ample parking are located at regular intervals along this stretch of highway. All trails are less than a quarter mile in length.

At Ruby Beach, the highway bends inland and enters the lower reaches of the Hoh Valley. Approximately 12 miles inland it crosses the Hoh River. Hoh Oxbow Campground is located here, operated by the Washington State Department of Natural Resources.

OIL CITY

Oil City lives up to neither parts of its name. The natural petroleum seeps discovered near the Hoh River, led to hopes, in the early part of this century, that the area could be commercially exploited. But the hopes were unfulfilled and the city never came to be. The 12-mile road to Oil City, paved for about 9 miles, leaves U.S. 101 a half-mile north of the highway bridge over the Hoh River and ends on a bluff overlooking the mouth of the river.

HOH RAIN FOREST

About 1½ miles north of the Hoh River bridge, the Hoh Road heads inland from U.S. 101. This road is paved for its entire 19-mile length. Along the way it passes

Continued on page 32

EXPLORING THE RAIN FORESTS

Western Hemlock

The uncommon alchemy of abundant rainfall, broad, glacier-carved river valleys, and an undisturbed forest ecosystem produces one of the temperate zone's most unusual forests: the Olympic rain forest. Significant remnants of this forest ecosystem are found in Olympic National Park and Olympic National Forest. The Hoh, Queets, and Quinault river valleys each support rain forests that are accessible to the motorist. In each, towering conifers mingle with stately hardwoods and myriad other plant forms to create a confusing array of foliage.

The dark shafts of spruce, fir, and hemlock trunks contrast sharply with the graceful arching boughs of bigleaf and vine maple, which are upholstered with clubmoss and ferns. Alder flats along the river's edge represent the youngest of the rain forest tree communities. Grasses carpet the fertile, river-laid soil among the open stands. In the deeper recesses of the older forest, young Sitka spruce, western hemlock, and redcedar grope skyward toward the patches of sunlight breaking through the outstretched limbs.

The moist odor of decay mixes with the crisp aroma of conifer needles. Seedlings gain a precarious toehold in the spongelike debris of rotting stumps and downed logs, resulting in stiltlike roots that entangle the mossy hulks of long-dead giants or in collonades—straight rows of trees that draw moisture and nutrients from decaying nurse logs. Lichens, liverworts, clubmoss, and ferns thrive in this lush forest, clinging to limbs of living trees and gathering airborne moisture carried in rain and fog.

Animal life is plentiful in the rain forest. In early spring, tiny winter wrens perch on the rootwads of windthrown trees, attracting mates with their song. In fall, bull Roosevelt elk bellow their haunting "bugle," the signal that attracts the females. River otters pursue fingerling salmon in the backwaters and beaver ponds of the rain forest floodplain. Flying squirrels glide from tree to tree in the night stillness of the rain forest canopy.

Several interpretive facilities provide information about the Olympic rain forest. The Hoh Visitor Center, with its museum, bookstore, and nature trails, is 19 miles off U.S. 101 on the Hoh Road, at the Hoh Campground and Ranger Station in Olympic National Park. The U.S. Forest Service operates an information center at the Quinault Ranger District headquarters on the South Shore Road of Quinault Lake.

Western Redcedar

several relatively undeveloped Department of Natural Resources (DNR) campgrounds, a gas station and store, and numerous farms. After about 13 miles, the road enters the park. The road meanders gently through the spectacular forest and ends at the Hoh Campground, Visitor Center, and Ranger Station. The visitor center features exhibits that help prepare hikers for the nature trails just outside. Books, maps, and other information are also available. Two nature trails, the Hall of Mosses and Spruce Bottom, wind through the giant spruces, hemlocks, and maples that characterize this temperate jungle.

The campground has 95 sites, many of which are suitable for trailers and RVs up to 21 feet long. Naturalist-led campfire programs and walks are conducted between July 1 and Labor Day.

BOGACHIEL RIVER

Highway 101 crosses the Bogachiel River 7 miles north of the Hoh Road and 6 miles south of the town of Forks. Bogachiel State Park is situated on the river, just west of the highway. It includes 41 sites, a dump station, and showers. A store and gas station are nearby. The Bogachiel Road cuts along the bluff overlooking the highway bridge and heads upvalley. There are no established campgrounds in this part of the valley. The trailhead for the Bogachiel River trail into Olympic National Park is located 5 miles up the valley just off the unimproved logging road. Hikers able to negotiate the first 3 miles (outside the park and thus rarely maintained) can walk up the Bogachiel Valley, and come out at Soleduck Hot Springs, a distance of 27 miles.

LA PUSH, AT THE MOUTH OF THE Quillayute River, may have gotten its name from *la bouche*, French for "the mouth." The harbor has sheltered a history of small fleets, from the canoes of early native seal and whale hunters to the fishing boats that now ply the offshore waters. This view is from 1924. (*Opposite*) The moody Olympic coast—a tenuous calm between the squalls.

FORKS

Located on a prairie near the confluence of the Bogachiel and Calawah rivers, the town of Forks boasts one of the most enthusiastic Fourth of July celebrations in the Northwest. Motels, restaurants, sporting goods stores, grocery stores, gas stations, auto repair services, and river-fishing guides are all available. The Forks Timber Museum, near Tillicum Park, displays logging equipment and other memorabilia from the bustling days of yesteryear. Also nearby is the Olympic Area Headquarters for the State Department of Natural Resources, which can supply information about DNR campsites and recreation areas.

The Forks Joint Information Center, cooperatively managed by Olympic National Forest and Olympic National Park, is 4 miles north of town on U.S. 101. Stop here for information, books, and maps pertaining to areas operated by either agency.

LA PUSH AND MORA

Downriver from Forks, the Bogachiel and Soleduck rivers combine to form the Quillayute River. At its mouth is the fishing village of La Push, the traditional home and reservation center of the Quileute tribe. Across the river mouth from La Push is Rialto Beach, a picnic site included in the Mora area of Olympic National Park. To reach Mora and La Push, turn west off Highway 101 at the La Push Road, about 2 miles north of Forks. After 8 miles, the road forks, with one branch going to La Push and the other to Mora and beyond, to Rialto Beach.

The left fork leads to La Push, 6 miles down the road. En route, two trailheads adjoin the road. The first is the mile-long Third Beach trail, about 12 miles from U.S. 101. The second is located about 1½ miles farther. This half-mile trail leads to Second Beach, where views of rugged islands and sea-stacks make the short hike a memorable one. La Push has restaurants, motels, grocery stores, and gas stations.

Mora and Rialto Beach are reached by following the right-hand fork in the La Push Road and crossing the one-lane Soleduck River bridge just beyond. Mora Campground is 12 miles off the highway and has 91 sites and an RV dump station. Park naturalists conduct campfire programs and daily guided tidepool walks during the summer season. Mora also has a ranger station; information about beach hikes and tide schedules can be obtained there.

Rialto Beach is 2 miles beyond Mora and has a picnic area and restrooms. Popular short hikes that begin here include Hole-in-the-Wall (a wave-carved tunnel in the rocks), a mile away, and the Chilean Memorial, 2½ miles up the beach. The memorial commemorates the loss of twenty lives on November 29, 1920, when the schooner *W.J. Pirrie* was shipwrecked.

POINTS NORTH AND EAST

North of Forks, U.S. 101 sweeps to the east and follows the Soleduck River Valley toward Lake Crescent and Port Angeles. At Sappho, the highway is joined by Burnt Mountain Road, a time-saving paved road that connects with Clallam Bay, the Strait of Juan de Fuca, and Neah Bay.

HOMESTEADERS SETTLED MOST of the peninsula's river valleys, hewing rough openings in the forest large enough to graze a few cattle and raise some potatoes. The Fred Fisher farm (*opposite*) was one of the many that flourished, but only briefly—few settlers endured the isolation and gloom of the rain-soaked country for very long.

STRAIT OF JUAN DE FUCA

FABLED STRAIT

The clouds had lifted by the time I reached the cape. After a half-mile scramble through the undergrowth along a muddy trail, I reached a place where the sound of the waves was louder. The trees in this little forest were dwarfish — windblown by cold breezes that had found something living to rub against after thousands of miles of bare Pacific. The stiff needles of the Sitka spruce hissed softly as they raked the salty breath.

I descended to a flat spot where the trees opened up a bit. Waist-high islands of dense shrubbery surrounded me, but the view opened completely. To the sides, waves funneled into frothy slots in the stubborn headland. In front of me, the prow of the continent hung over cold seawater, undercut by the violent waves that scoured the rocks below. Beyond by half a mile, Tatoosh Island seemed to float at anchor, an awkward naval redoubt under oceanic siege; its lighthouse and horn marked it dutifully.

With suppressed excitement, I found the most prominent flat spot that offered secure footing and stood on it. I took in a sweeping view of the distant horizon and, having completed the arc, turned to see the land. For some reason, I expected the Olympic Peninsula to look different from the very tip of its most northwestern extremity. The absurdity of that prospect sunk in abruptly, however—all I could see was a few hundred feet of heavily shrubbed forest. No sense of the whole appeared. I couldn't see the peninsula for the trees.

In his 1778 diary, Captain James Cook remarked upon a cape that "flattered us with the hopes of finding a harbour." No harbor found, he lay well offshore, and when a squall arose, he put to sea. He smugly remarked that the "pretended strait of Juan de Fuca" allegedly lay somewhere nearby but that he "saw nothing like it; nor is there the least probability that any such thing existed." On that point, Cook flattered himself.

A strait indeed existed and exists today at 48 degrees, 30 minutes north latitude. It cleaves the western shore of the continent with more authority than any of the big rivers. It forms the entrance to Puget Sound and the Strait of Georgia—the inland seas of Washington State and the Province of British Columbia. The rumor of Cook's time, however, was that "de Fuca's Strait" was the western entrance to the Straits of Anian—the mythical Northwest Passage—the shortcut from the Atlantic to the riches of the Pacific and the Orient.

The uncharted coasts of the Pacific Northwest presented each of the major world powers of the day with grand prospects. The English wanted to substantiate the claims of Sir Francis Drake, who had veered northward along the California coast (perhaps even the Washington coast) in 1577 on his voyage around the world. The Spanish were eager to make good on the claim of Balboa, who waded into the Pacific at the Isthmus of Panama in 1513 and claimed, for Spain, the entire Pacific Ocean and all the shores it lapped against. Real or supposed commercial riches and the opportunity to dominate the world's oceans sparked intense rivalries among nations and navigators. News of discovery was either muffled in secrecy or ballyhooed with embellishment.

So it was that the tale of Apostolos Valerianos, a Greek ship's pilot nicknamed Juan de Fuca by his Spanish employers, made its way into seafarers' lore. In 1625, the story was published in which Juan de Fuca claimed that in 1592 he had sailed northward from the New Spain port of Acapulco into the Strait of Anian and after 20 days had reached the Atlantic. At that point, according to his story, he backtracked to Acapulco. The story, as with other similar tales, had its supporters and its skeptics, and whether as detractors or corroborators, navigators marked the intersection of the forty-eighth parallel and the western coast of the continent as a point that bore further investigation.

Because of Cook's oversight, credit for the European discovery of the strait is most commonly bestowed upon Captain Charles Barkley, an English trader who, in addition to conducting a lucrative business voyage, was on a honeymoon cruise. Just prior to his departure from Europe in command of the *Imperial Eagle*, Barkley had wed sixteen-year-old Frances Hornby Trevor. The newlyweds crossed the Atlantic, rounded the horn, and made a stop in Hawaii. From there, they pressed for Nootka Sound to load sea-otter skins. Following a successful stop at Nootka, the *Imperial Eagle* probed the Vancouver Island coast, discovering Clayoquot and Barkley sounds—and the fabled Strait of Juan de Fuca. It is Mrs. Barkley's diary that records the event:

THE NORTHERN EDGE
FABLED STRAIT

0   5   10   15

◆ Information Centers
◇ Seasonal Information
   Centers
△ Campgrounds
▲ State Parks
--- Ferry Routes

Victoria

STRAIT OF JUAN DE FUCA

Cape Flattery

Neah Bay

Shi-Shi Beach

Cape Alava

Ozette

112   Sekiu

Clallam Bay

Widbey Island

Burnt Mtn. Road

Ozette L.

Sappho

Fairholm

Lyre R.

Joyce

112

Port Angeles

Dungeness Spit

Dungeness

Quimper Peninsula

Ft. Worden S.P.

Keystone

Port Townsend

Ft. Flagler S.P.

Soleduck R.

Lake Crescent

Soleduck Hot Springs

Heart O' the Hills

Hurricane Ridge Rd.

Sequim

20

Sequim Bay S.P.

Forks

101

Deer Park

Dungeness R.

104

La Push

Hoh Rd.

Hoh R.

Olympic National Park

Elwha R.

Olympic National Park

101

Kingston

In the afternoon, to our great astonishment, we arrived off a large opening extending to the eastward, the entrance of which appeared to be about four leagues wide, and remained about that width as far as the eye could see, with a clear westerly horizon, which my husband immediately recognized as the long lost strait of Juan de Fuca, and to which he gave the name of the original discoverer, my husband placing it on his chart.

Although intrigued, Barkley was not sufficiently impressed to venture within the strait and chose to make for Macao, where he could sell his furs and gather his profit.

Subsequent visits to the Strait of Juan de Fuca were made by the English trader John Meares in 1788, American trader Captain Robert Gray in 1789, and the Spaniards Quimper and Eliza in 1790 and 1791, respectively.

The most detailed study of the strait and its inner branches was made by Captain George Vancouver, who entered it on a bright April day in 1792, commanding Cook's former ship, *Discovery*, and accompanied by an armed tender, the *Chatham*. His navigation and cartographic skills honed by years as a junior officer on Cook's voyages, Vancouver sought to explore and chart the Northwest coast— particularly "the supposed straits of De Fuca." Vancouver's method was to stay to the continental, or right-hand, shore, probing every inlet and sighting from every headland. So it was that he was the first navigator to chart the complete shoreline of the Olympic Peninsula. From a portable observatory at Discovery Bay he calculated the longitude using celestial bodies, and from

NEAH BAY AS IT APPEARED IN 1926. The bay is located along a broad beach just inside the entrance to the Strait of Juan de Fuca. It has sheltered, from time immemorial, a small fleet of vessels used by the Makah's for fishing, whaling, and trade. (*Opposite*) Today's fishing fleet based at Neah Bay consists of larger, more sophisticated craft, equipped to spend several days at sea trolling for salmon.

longboats rowed along the shore he affixed accurate positions to the capes and coves of the strait and Hood Canal and discovered a major body of water to the southeast—now known as Puget Sound.

Today, the Strait of Juan de Fuca offers the visitor the same beauty and opportunity to explore as it did in Vancouver's day. The accessibility of the upland, however, increases the exploratory activities that the modern discoverer can enjoy.

STATE ROUTE 112
State 112 is a two-lane paved road that connects the towns scattered along the Strait of Juan de Fuca between Neah Bay and Port Angeles. Going is sometimes slow, because of the winding road and few passing zones. Numerous scenic vistas of the strait and Vancouver Island open up to the motorist along the way. Be sure to pull off the road to take in the sights—it's safer.

U.S. 101
U.S. 101 stays inland along the northern stretch of the peninsula, connecting Forks and points south with Port Angeles, Sequim, and points east. In spite of its winding route along the shore of Lake Crescent, it is quicker than State 112 for getting between Clallam Bay and Port Angeles.

NEAH BAY
The community of Neah Bay is in the extreme northwest corner of the peninsula, 70 miles west of Port Angeles. Groceries and gas are available, as well as overnight accommodations and restaurants. Numerous charter boat operations are based here.

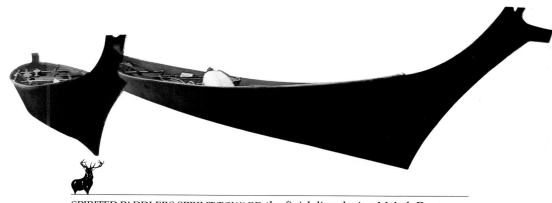

SPIRITED PADDLERS SPRINT TOWARD the finish line during Makah Days canoe races at Neah Bay (*opposite*). Tribes throughout the Puget Sound region send crews to these traditional meets. (*Above*) Salmon cooked in the traditional fashion acquire the smoky flavor of slow-burning alder wood. Ocean-going canoes hand-hewn out of cedar are displayed at the Makah Museum on the Makah Indian Reservation.

Catches include salmon, lingcod, rockfish, and halibut.

The Makah Museum, with its excellent exhibits, gives visitors a rare look into the culture of the Makah people. Many of the artifacts have come from archaeological digs near Ozette, about 14 miles south along the outer coast, and the Hoko River mouth, about 15 miles east, along the strait.

Day hikes to Shi-Shi Beach and Cape Flattery begin at trailheads several miles southwest of town. To reach them, follow the signs to Makah Air Force Station (communications only, no runways). At the station, the road forks. To reach Shi-Shi ("shy-shy"), turn to the left and follow the muddy road to its end. Parking areas are subject to change. Shi-Shi is about a 3-mile hike. To reach Cape Flattery, take the right-hand fork at the Air Force station and continue along the gravel road about 4 miles. Park in a muddy turnoff and walk down the old roadbed to the left. Cape Flattery is a half-mile away, over a primitive, sometimes slippery footpath.

SEKIU AND CLALLAM BAY

Farther east along the strait are neighboring towns of Sekiu ("see-cue") and Clallam Bay, 13 and 17 miles from Neah Bay, respectively. Motels, grocery stores, gas stations, fishing charters, and several marinas are located along this stretch of State 112. The Slip Point Lighthouse, completed in 1905, is at Clallam Bay.

OZETTE LAKE

Ozette Lake is the largest natural freshwater body in Washington State. It lies just inland from the coast, at the end of the Hoko Road, about 25 miles southwest of Sekiu. The Hoko Road is paved, but may have a few gravel stretches as the result of occasional slides. Located within the park boundaries, Ozette Lake offers superb boating, with miles of marshy shoreline and a boat-in campsite.

Park facilities at the lake include a ranger station, 22-site campground, summer interpretive programs, and hiking trails. Many hikers undertake the 10-mile, three-sided loop around the lake to the coast as a day hike. Others hike only one leg or stay overnight at campsites along the coast. Because of the unique hazards of beach hiking, it is a good idea to consult tide tables and to check in at the ranger station before hitting the trails.

BURNT MOUNTAIN ROAD

This road is a time saver. It connects State Route 112, 6 miles east of Clallam Bay, with Highway 101 at Sappho, making the trip from Port Angeles to Neah Bay faster than if one stays on State Route 112.

LOWER SOLEDUCK VALLEY

Between Sappho and Lake Crescent, U.S. 101 crosses the meandering Soleduck River several times, giving the motorist glimpses of this broad, cobbled river known for its steelhead and salmon runs. Bear Creek campground (20 sites), operated by the Washington Department of Natural Resources, is located 4 miles east of Sappho. The Soleduck Hatchery of the Washington Department of Fisheries has interpretive displays for visitors and is located just off U.S. 101, approximately 8 miles east of Sappho. Klahowya Campground (U.S. Forest Service) is about 15 miles east of Sappho and has 40 sites.

JOYCE

Along Route 112 is Joyce, a small logging community with a rich local history. Early town sites just north of Joyce, along the strait, took advantage of compact harbors and, for a short time, were prosperous ports. A railroad once passed through Joyce's heart, and the former depot is now a small museum. Groceries and gas are available at a combination general store and post office. Nearby is a State Department of Natural Resources campground at the Lyre River.

The paved but winding Piedmont Road,

STEEL WILLS AND RAZOR SHARP SAWBLADES subdued the wild Olympic forests. A falling team (*opposite*) pauses with the tools of their trade—the springboard, misery whip, and the doublebit axe. (*Above*) Rust and overgrown rights-of-way are the only remnants of the Olympic logging railroad heritage. The whistles of engines and the hiss of steam-powered donkeywinches slowly gave way to the whine of diesel.

AUTOMOBILES PUT WHEELS UNDER AMERICANS and the "frontier" within their reach. Auto camps, such as this one at La Poel on Lake Crescent, promoted outdoor recreation that was both rustic and civilized. Given the roads of the old days, such "luxury" remained adventurous. (*Opposite*) Pyramid Peak rises out of the deep water of Lake Crescent. Glaciers gnawing at the Olympic bedrock carved this and many other lake basins. Resistant ridges and outcrops create dramatic relief and spectacular views. The lake and the Strait of Juan de Fuca are visible from the summit of Pyramid Peak; a trail leads to its summit.

which branches off State 112 at the Crescent schoolgrounds, leads to East Beach on Lake Crescent, 4½ miles "over the hump." Along the strait, Salt Creek Recreation Area, operated by Clallam County, sits on the grounds of a former shore artillery battery, Camp Hayden. Salt Creek features a marine life sanctuary, with kelp beds and tidepools, and an 83-site campground.

LAKE CRESCENT AND SOLEDUCK

Located within Olympic National Park, Lake Crescent and Soleduck are outstanding areas of scenic beauty, natural wonders, and historical significance. The hot spring at Soleduck has soothed many a traveler's tired muscles since the first resort was established there around the turn of the century, while the lure of its deep azure water and mighty trout has made Lake Crescent a tourist destination since the 1890s.

Set deep among the northern ridges of the Olympics, Lake Crescent offers picnic sites, resort accommodations, boat launches, miles of trails, and good fishing. Lake Crescent Lodge and Log Cabin Resort offer cabins, rooms, and dining. Overnight accommodations require several months' advance reservation, but cancellations frequently occur— call ahead to find out. Camp David Junior, located on the north shore within the park but operated by Clallam County, is available for group use by reservation. Groceries and gas are available at Fairholm at the west end of the lake, near the Fairholm Campground (National Park Service). Marymere Falls, a 90-foot tendril of falling water, is a

Continued on page 50

COUNTRY INNS & RESORTS

A s I turned for a last glimpse of the beautiful blue lake dissolving in the firs, I said to myself, 'This is surely hard to beat. Gem indeed of the Olympics, and worth three times the stay.'"
—H. F. Dodge, travel writer, 1903

Such sentiments have been written and uttered since the earliest days of settlement on the Olympic Peninsula. Intrepid visitors have been on the scene for at least as long as settled residents. One of the most magnetic of the peninsula's attractions is Lake Crescent—the "gem" of Mr. Dodge's heartfelt farewell.

Lake Crescent was considered a wonder from the time that trappers John Everett and John Sutherland stumbled across it in 1849. Its startling blue water and dramatic settling among lush forested mountain slopes gave it an other-worldly aura perfectly matched to Romantic-era images of Nature in her perfection.

Resorts lined the shores as early as the 1890s, catering to travelers from as far away as England who came here to breathe the fragrant air, enjoy casual fireside company, or catch the legendary Beardslee and Crescenti trout known to lurk in the deep water.

Present-day Lake Crescent Lodge is the only resort that still operates in its original building. The two-story shingle-covered lodge was constructed in time for the 1915 tourist season and was known as Singer's Lake Crescent Tavern. Outlying cabins supplemented the larger building for sleeping space. Dining was elegant, and activities included rowing, tennis, horseshoes, croquet, and trapshooting.

Lake Crescent Lodge's most prestigious guest was President Franklin D. Roosevelt, who stayed at the inn during his visit in October 1937. Following two days of negotiation in a lakeside cabin with several U.S. Senators and high officials of the U.S. Forest Service and National Park Service, Roosevelt became convinced that Olympic National Park should be created and enthusiastically endorsed a plan to increase the acreage in the proposed park. Though the presidential visit was short, its impact is still felt. On June 29, 1938, Congress established Olympic National Park. The "gem" remains secure.

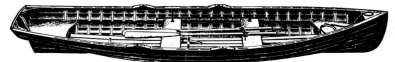

LAKE CRESCENT LODGE IS TYPICAL of the small inns and lodges run by concessionaires for the park. Concessionaires are licensed by the national park system; they supply accommodations for visitors at reasonable rates—cottages, lodge rooms, and cabins for example, many with lovely lake and mountain views. The park's lodges can boast good food and a variety of activities—ample fishing, nature walks, hikes, and especially on Lake Crescent, canoe rides.

¾-mile walk from the ranger station just east of Lake Crescent Lodge.

Soleduck is located 12 miles up the paved Soleduck Road, which meets U.S. 101 a mile west of the western tip of Lake Crescent. Because its campground is one of the most heavily used in Olympic National Park, plan to get there early in the day during summer. If the campground is full, try Fairholm Campground or, slightly west on U.S. 101, Klahowya Campground. The Sol Duc Resort has dining, cabins, hot baths, and a swimming pool. Several hiking trails radiate from the area, leading through the spectacular lowland forest valley or into the high country.

ELWHA VALLEY

The Elwha Valley, about 9 miles west of Port Angeles, is one of the most significant historical areas in Olympic National Park. Its lower reaches were settled late in the nineteenth century, and it was through this corridor that the Press Expedition of 1890 entered the heart of the Olympic Mountains. The Elwha Ranger Station was once the Forest Service headquarters for the administration of Mt. Olympus National Monument and, with the establishment of Olympic National Park, became park headquarters for a time. A Civilian Conservation Corps (CCC) camp was located here during the Depression.

Campgrounds include Elwha Campground, 3 miles off U.S. 101, with 23 sites, and Altaire Campground, 4½ miles from U.S. 101, with 29 sites. Elwha trailheads mark the start of hikes to Hurricane Ridge,

Low Divide (Press Expedition route), and other points in the Olympic back country.

PORT ANGELES

Set about midway along the strait, Port Angeles provides a convenient base for day trips to Hurricane Ridge, Victoria, B.C., and Dungeness Spit. Fairchild Airport offers both scheduled and charter flights. Scheduled flights to and from Port Angeles can connect with major airline flights out of Seattle-Tacoma International Airport at reasonable cost. Car rentals are available, and tour buses and public transit make outlying areas easily accessible. The town offers a broad range of motels, restaurants, grocery and sporting goods stores, laundromats, gas stations, auto repair shops, trailer and boating supply places, and fresh seafood outlets. Fishing charters for salmon are available. Public showers can be found at the public swimming pool, just a few blocks from downtown.

The Pioneer Memorial Museum, Olympic National Park's main interpretive center, is a must for park visitors. It is located on the Hurricane Ridge Road, just inside city limits. Exhibits, audiovisual programs, and a trained staff provide an excellent introduction to Olympic National Park. Books, maps, and brochures pertaining to the park can be obtained here.

The Clallam County Museum, next to the public library downtown, displays many exhibits on local history. The award-winning City Pier, on the waterfront, presents live marine biology exhibits at the Arthur Fiero Memorial Laboratory.

During the summer, the privately run

ferry *Coho* makes several roundtrip runs to Victoria each day; fall, winter, and spring schedules vary. Walk-on travel is the most hassle-free—taking a car can involve long waits (sometimes overnight). Ferry schedules are available at visitor information centers and many businesses. They can be obtained in advance by writing to Black Ball Transport, Inc., 106 Surrey Bldg., Bellevue, Washington 98004.

Other information about the Port Angeles area is available through the Chamber of Commerce information booth located near the waterfront as well as in the form of several locally published visitor guides, given out free in stores, motels, and other establishments.

HURRICANE RIDGE

Just 17 miles south of Port Angeles, Hurricane Ridge stands nearly a mile above sea level and offers spectacular views of the Olympic Mountains, the Strait of Juan de Fuca, and Vancouver Island. The wide, paved road winds steadily around the shoulder of Mount Angeles, providing several excellent vistas along the way. The grade is an even 7 percent that cars and motor homes can climb without problem. Motorists pulling trailers may find it more convenient to leave them in Port Angeles or at Heart O' the Hills, however. Camping is possible only at Heart O' the Hills Campground, 5 miles out of town; the ridge itself is open only to day use.

Visitor services at the ridge include a full schedule of interpretive activities led by park naturalists, exhibits in the lodge,

THE PORT ANGELES HARBOR, situated within the protective arm of Ediz
Hook, is home to a mixed fleet of work and pleasure boats. Large ocean-
going vessels also call here, picking up lumber products and transporting
them around the world. The auto-ferry *Coho* makes roundtrip runs to
Victoria, British Columbia each day.

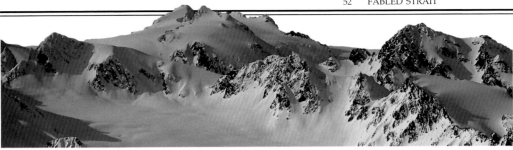

THE SEASONS OF THE OLYMPICS are vividly reflected on the mountain faces. Qualities of light, the movements of air, the shapes of clouds—all suggest the indelible stamp of seasonal variation. (*Opposite*) An aerial view of Mt. Olympus and its glacier-covered slopes. There are a surprising number of glaciers in Olympic National Park. Over 60 of these icefields move slowly down mountainsides, making changes that are gradual and far less dramatic than the seasons.

and a restaurant and gift store operated by a concessionaire. The numerous trails that crisscross the high meadows and ridges range from short, paved, handicap-accessible nature trails to more extensive paths along the rocky ridges. Wildflowers carpet the meadows and slopes in a tapestry that changes throughout the summer; avalanche and glacier lilies bloom in June and July, lupine and a host of others in July and August. Glaciers on Mount Carrie, Mount Olympus, and Mount Anderson are visible on clear days.

Hurricane Ridge is open for winter use when the weather allows the road to be plowed. Miles of cross-country ski trails offer outstanding high-country travel. A modest downhill ski area includes two rope tows and a poma lift. Snowshoe walks and winter survival demonstrations are conducted by naturalists.

DEER PARK
Another high-country view is available from Deer Park, on the slopes of Blue Mountain east of Hurricane Ridge. The Deer Park Road, which climbs 5400 feet in its 19-mile length, is unpaved and thus unsuitable for trailers and RVs. Deer Park Road joins U.S. 101 just east of the Port Angeles city limits. Deer Park Campground and Ranger Station (staffed during the summer) is located at road's end. The campground has 10 campsites.

SEQUIM-DUNGENESS VALLEY
The broad plain formed where the Dungeness River leaves the mountains is one of the few areas on the peninsula where grain, fruit, and seed crops are cultivated.

Located within the semi-arid lee of the Olympics, the Sequim area offers great variety to the casual visitor.

Dungeness Spit, one of the longest natural sand spits in the world, reaches far out into the strait, harboring within its thin arc an estuary teeming with shorebirds, migratory waterfowl, clams, oysters, and harbor seals. The spit itself is within the boundaries of the Dungeness National Wildlife Refuge—an outstanding resource for birdwatchers and students of shore-building processes. There is a campground operated by Clallam County at the base of the spit. To reach the spit from U.S. 101, turn north onto Kitchen Road, about 4 miles west of Sequim. Proceed about 3 miles and follow the road as it turns east. The entrance to Dungeness Recreation Area is on the left.

Paved country roads (excellent for bicycling) lead to the old town of Dungeness, several miles east of the spit base. The lighthouse on the end of the spit can be seen beyond the decaying pilings that once supported a half-mile-long dock. The town was the first seat of Clallam County.

Two local wineries, Neuharth and Lost Mountain, have put the Sequim Valley on the map for wine aficionados. Both wineries welcome visitors to their tasting rooms. Check local phone books for numbers and call for visiting hours and directions.

The Manis Mastodon Site, near Sequim, gives visitors a look back to a time when these elephantlike creatures roamed the Ice Age lowlands. Mastodon remains, unearthed in 1977, are on display. Open only during the summer months, the site is under systematic excavation; visitors may thus have the opportunity to see the operation in progress.

The Olympic Game Farm provides glimpses of exotic animals used in the filming of "wild" animal segments for movies, television programs, and commercials.

The town of Sequim, which straddles U.S. 101 17 miles east of Port Angeles, has several motels. Groceries, gas, and auto repair services are readily available. Other services include laundromats, a movie theater, restaurants, a historical museum, and a public library.

Several miles east of town lies Sequim Bay, with Sequim Bay State Park and the John Wayne Marina. Both have boat ramps. The state park has 119 sites, showers, picnic areas, and a dock. The park is quite popular during summer months, so it is best to arrive early to obtain a site.

Near Sequim Bay State Park, the Palo Alto Road leads toward the mountains. The road is paved for about 5 miles. Two U.S. Forest Service campgrounds, Dungeness Forks and East Crossing, lie tucked in the Dungeness River canyon, accessible only by narrow, winding roads. Numerous trails lead into the high country, parts of which are in the newly established Buckhorn Wilderness. Check Forest Service maps for road numbers and trailhead access.

PORT TOWNSEND
Port Townsend sits on the Quimper Peninsula, 12 miles off U.S. 101 on State Route 20. Originally intended as a major railroad terminus and commercial metropolis, Port Townsend sports all the gingerbread trim-

A THIN RIND OF ICE encases a leaf fallen from a bigleaf maple. (*Opposite*) The Dungeness Valley has long supported farming. Dairy products, vegetable seed, cane berries, and hay are the most common crops. Located to leeward of the mountains, less than 16 inches of annual rainfall is often recorded, making it the driest area on the Pacific coast north of San Diego, in extreme southern California.

mings that accompanied its 1870s boom-town optimism. A significant portion of the early history of the peninsula was played out here during the city's heyday as a seaport and business center. Much of the architecture of that period has been restored, including not only the typical Victorian style but other styles as well, making the town an engrossing study for fans of old buildings. In a town that is itself a museum, the Jefferson County Historical Museum is of special interest.

Port Townsend has also established a reputation for hosting regional and national festivals for jazz, fiddle music, dance, wooden boats, painting, and writing. Festival information can be obtained from the Chamber of Commerce.

Port Townsend offers overnight accommodations that range from homey bed and breakfasts, to grander period hotels and modern motels, to historic officers' quarters. Campsites can be found at nearby Fort Worden State Park. Youth hostels are operated at both Fort Worden and Fort Flagler state parks. A number of specialty restaurants cater to differing tastes and budgets. Picnic lunches can be assembled from any of several downtown delis and taken to places along the waterfront or to Chetzemoka Park, named for an important Klallam chief. Boutiques and bookstores, art galleries and antique shops offer many interesting items for shoppers.

Port Townsend is also a vital ferry link to Whidbey Island and points east and north across Puget Sound. Frequent sailings in the summer help ease congestion, but it is wise to show up several hours before departure.

MANY OF PORT TOWNSEND'S Victorian-style homes—built during the town's historic boom, when hopes were high for a railroad terminus—have been lost, including the James House shown here. Restorers have preserved, however, much of the architecture that today reveals the opulence and optimism of a bygone era. (*Opposite*) Port Townsend was, for a time, Washington's premier seaport. During its heyday, merchant ships, whalers, and warships frequently anchored there, and folklore of the period includes tales of sailors forcefully or unknowingly recruited from local saloons.

MOUNT ANDERSON

THE EASTERN SIDE

STEEP RIVERS

Viewed from the east side of Puget Sound, the Olympics form an imposing wall. The teeth and notches of their silhouetted crest form the measuring marks against which the season can be gauged according to sunset. In winter, the long-shadowed light casts brilliance upon the snow-dusted peaks, making them dance against the gunmetal sky. In summer the snow, bathed in hot light, retreats into narrow creases on the cool north side.

A drive or hike into the Olympics from the Hood Canal side illustrates just how steeply the mountain canyons rise from saltmarsh to snowpatch. Mountain trails climb over such obstacles as "Big Hump" in the Duckabush and "Heart Attack Hill" in the Dosewallips. Narrow, winding roads cling to canyon walls, and frothy rivers thunder among the boulders that line their steep beds. Ravines that in winter are rights-of-way for avalanches grow thick with slide-alder underbrush in summer.

The steepness of this country comes home when I remember my first visit to Staircase Rapids on the Skokomish River in Olympic National Park. The rapids are impressive throughout the year: Cataracts plunge among massive boulders; Dolly Varden trout lie in the deep pools. But on this occasion the rapids were particularly awesome. A September storm had dropped an inch of rain in just under 24 hours—an abnormal abundance for the dry side of the peninsula. Downstream, the river was rising quickly. By midday whole trees, roots intact and bark scraped off in large patches, were careening in the current, spinning lengthwise in the eddies. The river was a creamy brown— like coffee laced with too much half and

half, thickened with too much sugar. As I walked the half-mile up the trail to the rapids, it actually seemed that the earth was shaking. At the rapids themselves, most of the truck-sized boulders were nearly covered with water. The rapids were one long chute of surging water, not the separate pools and cascades of the river at its normal stage. The steep river made its own thunder—even shouting was insufficient to overcome the din. I saw the trees—70-foot matchsticks—as they entered the tumult. They would vanish, only to reappear hundreds of feet downstream, bobbing to the surface when the sucking current released them.

The rainstorm had entered the mountains suddenly, and the runoff was leaving the mountains just as suddenly. Without the sheer quantity of absorptive plants and soil that characterize the west side, this tilted country shed the rainfall as fast as gravity would carry it.

The steepness of this country also made a lasting impression on its first explorers. In the summer of 1890, Lieutenant Joseph P. O'Neil led an expedition jointly organized by the U.S. Army and the Oregon Alpine Club into the eastern Olympics to survey the maze of valleys, ridges, and peaks. In contrast to the highly sensationalized Press Expedition that had penetrated the Elwha River valley the previous winter, the O'Neil expedition proceeded quietly and efficiently and was well prepared to document the new territory scientifically. The party was ferried by steamboat to a settlement at Lilliwaup, on Hood Canal, and proceeded overland to Lake Cushman. From there, they slowly

moved up the north fork of the Skokomish, carving a trail along the canyon walls and through the sometimes impenetrable vegetation.

In his diary account of the expedition, Private Harry Fisher wrote:

Pushing on, we discovered fresh elk tracks and followed them perhaps two mile, finding a route in that manner, that we might never have otherwise discovered, through the ugliest portion of the canyon. Many mountain streams came in here and numerous springs, making the earth soft and miry and undergrowth more rank. A narrow bottom bordered the stream upon one side or the other, with a growth of large alders and a variety of brush and elk ferns beneath. For hours we battled against this, and a rain set in to make it worse. We had to ride them down with our weight and were sometimes compelled to use hatchets to get through at all.

Against such tough going, the expedition wound through the valleys and passes and succeeded not only in mapping much of the region but in discovering a new species of mountain flower, the Olympic rockmat. As he assessed the wild land his exploring party had conquered, Lieutenant O'Neil later reported prophetically, ". . . while the country on the outer slope of these mountains is valuable, the interior is useless for all practical purposes. It would, however, serve admirably for a national park." Thus, the ruggedness of the land, its profusion of scenery and splendor but dearth of other exploitables, was seen by one of its first official spectators as fit for

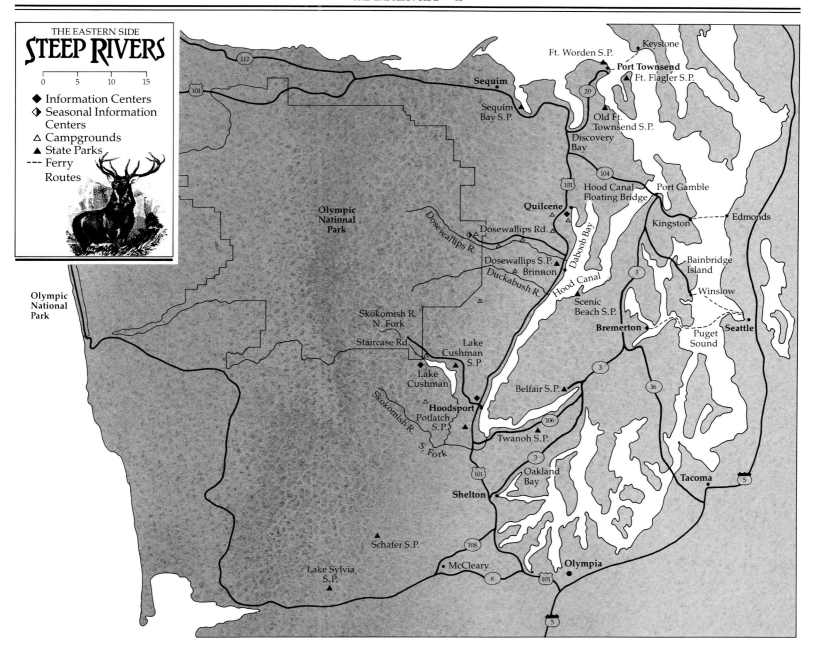

THE EASTERN SIDE

STEEP RIVERS

0   5   10   15

◆ Information Centers
◇ Seasonal Information
   Centers
△ Campgrounds
▲ State Parks
--- Ferry
    Routes

Keystone

Ft. Worden S.P.

Port Townsend
▲ Ft. Flagler S.P.

Sequim

20

Sequim
Bay S.P.

Old Ft.
Townsend S.P.

Discovery
Bay

104

101   Hood Canal
       Floating Bridge   Port Gamble

Quilcene

Kingston   Edmonds

Dosewallips Rd.

Dosewallips R.

Daboob Bay

Bainbridge
Island

Dosewallips S.P.
Brinnon

Duckabush R.

Hood Canal

Winslow

3

Scenic
Beach S.P.

Olympic
National
Park

Skokomish R.
N. Fork

Bremerton

Seattle

Staircase Rd.

Lake
Cushman
S.P.

Puget
Sound

Olympic
National
Park

Lake
Cushman

Belfair S.P.

3

Hoodsport
Potlatch
S.P.

16

106

Skokomish R. S. Fork

Twanoh S.P.

3

Oakland
Bay

Tacoma

5

101

Shelton

Schafer S.P.

108

Olympia

Lake Sylvia
S.P.

McCleary

8

101

5

enjoyment by future generations in its untouched form.

Today, the east side of the Olympics retains much of the character that the O'Neil expedition encountered. In addition, the combination of Hood Canal shoreline and mountain high country gives the east side some of the region's most varied scenery. Secluded coves on Hood Canal can provide moody walks along the cobblestone beaches or clamming and oyster gathering on the broad tidal flats. Scuba divers can gather bountiful catches of fish, molluscs, and octopus from the cold water of the canal. The river valleys offer picnic sites and campgrounds amid towering firs and wild rhododendrons. Scenic viewpoints provide sweeping vistas of mountains on one side and Hood Canal and the Puget lowland on the other. Scattered along the canal front, commercial shellfish growers sell their harvests of oysters, crabs, and hardshell clams from shops and stands.

The narrow band of lowland that separates the Olympics from Hood Canal may have cramped the extent of settlement and civilization, but it frees the traveler to smell fresh salt air within earshot of the rush of steep rivers.

DISCOVERY BAY

Discovery Bay marks the point where several important highways merge heading to points on and off the peninsula. At the head of the bay, State Route 20 originates, leading 12 miles toward Port Townsend,

the Keystone ferry and Whidbey Island, the Skagit Valley, and the North Cascades beyond. About 3 miles farther south, State Route 104 joins U.S. 101, forming the eastward link to the Hood Canal Floating Bridge and Puget Sound ferries at either Kingston or Winslow on Bainbridge Island.

THE HOOD CANAL FLOATING BRIDGE

Buoyed by the success of the first Lake Washington floating bridge in Seattle, state engineers completed the Hood Canal Bridge in 1961, eliminating an old ferry crossing and improving the highway access to the peninsula. In 1979, high winds severed the highway tie, sinking the western portion of the span. The bridge has since been reconstructed (with design improvements) and again links the Olympic Peninsula with the Kitsap Peninsula and the rest of civilization. A toll is charged for vehicles and bicycles.

Near the toll plaza on the eastern end, Highway 104 meets State Route 3, which leads south toward the Winslow and Bremerton ferries to Seattle. Highway 104 continues east through Port Gamble, a historic sawmill town, and on to Kingston, where ferries cross to Edmonds, a northern suburb of Seattle. Eastbound travelers aiming for points north and east of Seattle should consider this route—it connects conveniently with Interstate 5.

QUILCENE

Quilcene is slightly inland from Dabob Bay, one of the northern spurs of Hood Canal. The town has gas stations, auto repair facilities, food, lodging, groceries, and laundries. The U.S. Forest Service

headquarters for the Quilcene Ranger District is just south of town along Highway 101; stop there for information and maps. Nearby, there are several county and Forest Service campgrounds and picnic areas. Mount Walker viewpoint, about 5 miles south of Quilcene, offers views of both the Olympics and the Puget Sound lowland. The 5-mile dirt road that coils up the side of Mount Walker is not recommended for trailers. Showy rhododendrons are abundant on the slopes of Mount Walker through the late spring months.

DOSEWALLIPS

The town of Brinnon lies along Highway 101 near the mouth of the Dosewallips River. Services include gas, groceries, and restaurants. A short distance from Brinnon is Dosewallips State Park, which straddles the highway along the river. Seal Rock Campground, operated by the Forest Service, is north of town about 2 miles. Clamming and oyster picking are permitted there. From Brinnon, the Dosewallips Road leads into the mountains, passing the Elkhorn and Steelhead campgrounds (U.S. Forest Service) before it enters Olympic National Park. Dosewallips Ranger Station (staffed during the summer) and Campground are at the road's end, 15½ miles from Highway 101. The Dosewallips trail leads into the mountains, branching into two forks a mile and a half upvalley. One fork connects with Enchanted Valley; the other, with the Elwha River valley.

About 3 miles south of Brinnon along Highway 101 the Duckabush River Road

ROYAL BASIN in late summer in the eastern Olympics high country.

FOR MOST EARLY VISITORS, overnight trips into the wilderness were taken on horseback. Although many trails are maintained to accommodate horses, backpacking is now the most popular mode of travel. (*Opposite*) One of the Mildred Lakes in the Buckhorn Wilderness Area of Olympic National Forest. Accessible only by scrambling five miles over rough terrain on a primitive footpath, Mildred Lakes reveal the qualities that make the Olympic wilderness so compelling and mysterious.

winds into the mountains. The road is paved for the first 3 miles. At Interrorem Picnic Area, the blacktop ends. About 2 miles beyond is Camp Collins, a Forest Service campground. The road climbs another 2 miles to the Duckabush trailhead. From there, the Duckabush trail leads into The Brothers Wilderness Area and Olympic National Park.

HAMMA HAMMA
About 10 miles south of Brinnon, the Hamma Hamma Road joins U.S. 101. This road leads almost 16 miles into the mountains. Two Forest Service campgrounds are situated along the way: Hamma Hamma, 6 miles off U.S. 101, with 12 sites, and Lena Creek, 8½ miles off the highway, with 14 sites. Trails in the vicinity include the Lena Lakes trail and the Mildred Lakes trail into the heart of the newly established Mount Skokomish Wilderness Area.

HOODSPORT AND STAIRCASE
The town of Hoodsport is tucked in a shallow bay along Hood Canal. Gas, lodging, food, and groceries are available. Of particular interest here is the Hoodsport Salmon Hatchery, operated by the Washington State Department of Fisheries. The Hoodsport Winery sits beside Highway 101 just south of town.

Hoodsport is also an important junction, with the Staircase Road joining 101 in the middle of town. Two blocks off 101 is the Hoodsport Joint Information Center, operated by the Forest Service and National Park Service. Stop here for books, maps, and campground and other information.

TUMBLING WATER SOUNDS
and the rush of cool air fill
a steep ravine. The old say-
ing, "In the Olympics,
there's a stream around
every bend in the trail," is
not universally true.
Streams occur just infre-
quently enough to be
delightful surprises.
(*Opposite top*) An early
camp at Anderson Pass,
the divide between the
Dosewallips and the East
Fork of the Quinault River.
(*Bottom*) "Pioneering" tech-
niques for camping have
been replaced by "low
impact" methods.
Advances in outdoor
equipment design allow
today's back country vis-
itors to be much lighter on
the land. Lightweight
stoves have replaced camp-
fires, which can burn a
decade's worth of tree
growth in minutes, and
leave barren, soilless scars
where nutrients are
already in short supply.

The Lake Cushman–North Fork Skokomish Road is paved to Lake Cushman State Park, 7½ miles from Hoodsport. Lake Cushman supplies water to the Tacoma City Light powerhouse on Hood Canal. Beyond the state park, the road is unpaved and continues to the national park boundary 15 miles from Hoodsport.

Staircase Campground and Ranger Station are 16 miles from Hoodsport. Naturalist programs are conducted between July 1 and Labor Day. The Four Stream trail leads a half-mile to Staircase Rapids. Other trails lead up the north fork of the Skokomish River and into the national park back country or into the rugged Mount Skokomish Wilderness Area.

THE GREAT BEND OF HOOD CANAL
Continuing south along Highway 101 from Hoodsport, Hood Canal hooks around to the east. The Skokomish Indian Reservation occupies a large tract of lowland along the southwest shore of the elbow. Potlatch State Park is 3 miles south of Hoodsport. Gas and groceries are available along the highway. In the center of the reservation, U.S. 101 meets State Route 106, which winds northeast along the shore of the hook of Hood Canal toward Bremerton and the ferries to Seattle. Near the end of Hood Canal's hook, highway connections can be made that lead to Tacoma. Heading south, U.S. 101 continues toward Shelton and Olympia.

Continued on page 70

FREE LUNCH
OYSTERS & CLAMS

Olympic Feast
Magnifique

ince prehistoric times, shellfish have been a staple in the diet of peninsula residents. Shell heaps have been found at all village sites of native inhabitants, and early settlers took advantage of shellfish resources by harvesting, canning, and exporting clams at many sites around the peninsula. Modern growers continue to provide succulent Olympic shellfish to gourmet tables throughout North America.

Visitors to the peninsula are rewarded with many opportunities to take shellfish for themselves. Clothed in raingear and hip boots and armed with a full array of shovels, rakes, and buckets, they dutifully spread over the exposed tidelands in darkness or daylight, rain or shine—whenever the tide table indicates a low tide. Catches include hardshell clams such as native littleneck, butter clam, horse clam, and geoduck ("gooey-duck"); the Japanese or Pacific oyster; and, when stocks are healthy, the razor clam.

Hardshell clams go by several names. "Steamer" clams include native and manila littlenecks and are distinguished by fine radiating and concentric markings. Butter clams have only concentric markings. The geoduck has the reputation of being the largest of all the native clams—and the most elusive as quarry. These monsters commonly achieve weights of more than 6 pounds and have siphons that often reach 2 feet in length.

The Olympia oyster, regarded to be the finest flavored of all west coast oysters, is now limited to a few bays near Olympia because of pollution. This diminutive native is available only commercially—and then at a premium price. Japanese or Pacific oysters can be picked at a number of public beaches along Hood Canal or purchased from growers.

Razor clams, once the economic staple of areas with broad beaches, have suffered from parasitic attacks that apparently coincided with the 1982–1983 El Niño warm ocean water event. Whether El Niño caused the devastating affliction and whether stocks will once again be strong enough for harvest remain unknown.

During summer months, clams and oysters from Puget Sound, the Strait of Juan de Fuca, and Hood Canal are subject to plankton blooms called "red tide," which can cause paralytic shellfish poisoning. Check locally about red tide before picking; commercial shellfish are certified safe.

State regulations govern sport harvesting of clams. Sporting goods outlets and most stores near clam grounds will have brochures on limits. If you go digging, remember to backfill holes and to avoid trespassing.

Bouillabaisse is a hotchpotch in a pot, and not only is it a marvelous mixture of flavors, it can also be wonderfully varied according to taste or situation. This serendipitous dish can be prepared right on the shore where clams and mussels are gathered, and some would say open air is a necessary ingredient.

To serve six: Heat ¼ cup olive oil in a large pot and cook the following for 5 minutes:

Garlic, 1 clove finely chopped	Leek, 1 diced
Celery, 1 stalk chopped	Thyme, ½ teaspoon
Onion, 1 small chopped	Bay leaf

Next, add the following and simmer at least 20 minutes:

Tomatoes, 2 cups pureed or crushed	Fennel seeds, ½ teaspoon
Dry white wine, 1 cup	Salt, pepper, and parsley to taste
Water, 1 cup (or clam juice)	

If you're not cooking over an open fire in the sea breeze and not limited to your own catch, take advantage of the available varieties of fresh seafood at the many local fish markets. The list below only suggests the creative ways this dish can be prepared. Creativity enhances the flavor.

Crab, cut into pieces	Scallops or clams, 12
Mussels, 12 scrubbed	Fish, 1 pound rockfish or cod

Once the seafood is added, cook an additional 15 minutes.
Bon Olympique!

Manila
Littleneck
Clam

Native
Littleneck
Clam

Butter Clam

Olympic Oyster

Pacific Japanese Oyster

SHELTON

The town of Shelton is just off U.S. 101, about 12 miles south of the junction with State Route 106. The older part of Shelton is on Oakland Bay, a narrow arm of South Puget Sound. Sawmills line the waterfront. Shelton's colorful past as a lumber town merges with its present; historic buildings are sprinkled throughout town, and during the summer, regular tours of Simpson Timber Company's modern-day mill are scheduled. Visitor services include motels, restaurants, grocery stores, and service stations. Headquarters for the Shelton Ranger District of Olympic National Forest are just off U.S. 101 on the north side of town. Information about Forest Service facilities can be obtained there.

U.S. 101 TO OLYMPIA

South of Shelton, U.S. 101 is a divided highway for the 17 miles to Olympia, the state capital, where it joins Interstate 5.

WEST TO THE COAST

Two important routes connect U.S. 101 with the coast: State Route 108, which ties into U.S. 101 6 miles south of Shelton, and State Route 8, which joins U.S. 101 14 miles south of Shelton and 6 miles northwest of Olympia. Route 108 is a meandering country road forming a shortcut 12 miles through the foothills to McCleary. Just west of McCleary it connects to Route 8, which is a brisk divided highway. Route 8 helps link both legs of U.S. 101, closing the Olympic loop.

FOR MORE INFORMATION

Forks Joint Information Center
National Park Service/U.S. Forest Service
Star Route 1, Box 185
Forks, WA 98331

Forks Chamber of Commerce
P. O. Box 300
Forks, WA 98331

Grays Harbor Tourism Council
2109 Sumner Avenue, Suite 20
Aberdeen, WA 98520

Hoodsport Joint Information Center
National Park Service/U.S. Forest Service
P. O. Box 68
Hoodsport, WA 98548

Olympic National Park
600 East Park Avenue
Port Angeles, WA 98362

Olympic Peninsula Tourism Council
P. O. Box 303
Port Angeles, WA 98362

Port Townsend Chamber of Commerce
2437 Simms Way
Port Townsend, WA 98368

Sequim—Dungeness Chamber of Commerce
P. O. Box 907
Sequim, WA 98382

Shelton Chamber of Commerce
P. O. Box 666
Shelton, WA 98584

Washington State Parks and Recreation Commission
7150 Cleanwater Lane, KY-11
Olympia, WA 98504

For casual visitors to the peninsula and for those who plan to explore the area in depth, one essential source of information is the excellent map prepared jointly by the park and forest service. Aside from the detailed rendering that includes topography, trails, paved and unpaved roads, rivers, creeks and every landmark imaginable, it lists recreation sites and their facilities, points of interest, and the area's ranger stations. The map is available on the peninsula but to make the most of your visit, it's a good idea to review it in advance. For a copy of the U.S. Department of Agriculture/Forest Service map of Olympic National Forest and Olympic National Park, write to the park, or to either the Forks or Hoodsport joint information centers, at the addresses listed on this page.

LOST RIVER VALLEY, Bailey Range from Lost Pass.

ABOUT THE AUTHOR

Robert Steelquist learned his way around the Olympic Peninsula from the inside out. For many years he worked as a trailhand in the Olympic back country. He now works as a teacher, naturalist, and writer, interpreting the ecology and environmental issues of the Olympic Peninsula to visitors and residents alike. He and his family live in a house they built near Blyn, Washington. This book is dedicated to his wife Jenny.

ABOUT WOODLANDS PRESS

The purpose of Woodlands Press is to develop and publish works that will celebrate the beauty of America's national heritage and the tireless efforts of those men and women who have labored to preserve it. The Press collaborates with the personnel and associations of the various national parks and monuments, the National Park Service, and outstanding scientific authorities. Founded by Tokyo-based publisher Robert White and the design firm of McQuiston and Daughter, Inc., Woodlands Press is a division of Robert White and Associates, San Francisco, California.

ABOUT THE ASSOCIATION

Pacific Northwest National Parks and Forests Association is a nonprofit organization that operates under authorization of the federal government and with the support of the National Park Service. The association is managed by a board of directors composed of community leaders. Its purpose is to support the interpretive and related visitor-service activities of Olympic National Park and other park and forest sites throughout the northwest. Interpretive programs include publishing, purchasing, and distribution of literature about the park, acquiring display materials and equipment for museums and exhibits, and supporting educational activities.

ACKNOWLEDGMENTS

The author thanks Hank Warren, Don Jackson, Smitty Parratt, and the Woodlands staff, for their careful review of manuscripts. Additional thanks are due to: Terry Duffy for design and production; editors Jackie Estrada and Frankie Wright; Kristie Paulson for production; Gail E. H. Evans for photo research; and to Marci Wellens of Woodlands Press. Special appreciation goes to Pat O'Hara for his encouragement.

Quotations were taken from Robert Wood's, *Across the Olympic Mountains: the Press Expedition, 1889–90,* and *Men, Mules and Mountains: Lieutenant O'Neil's Olympic Expeditions,* and were reprinted by permission of the Mountaineers.

PHOTOGRAPHY CREDITS

Pat O'Hara: front and back covers; 2, 4, 6, 18, 23, 26, 29, 30 (*bottom*), 31, 47, 51, 52, 53, 54, 55, 57, 58, 63, 65, 66, 70, and 71. Cindy McIntyre: 17, 36, 37, 40, 42, 43, and 59. Keith D. Lazelle: 19, 27, 28, 30 (*top*), and 33. Tom and Pat Leeson: 11. Tully Stroud: 12 (*top*). Ross Hamilton: 49. Karen Orsen: 69 (*bottom*). Photophile/Joe Craighead: 69 (*bottom*). Washington State Historical Society: 1, 12 (*bottom*), 13, 14–15 (*top*), 32, 35, 46, 48, 64, and 67. University of Washington: 7 and 22. Whatcom Museum of Art and History: 14–15 (*center*), 24–25 (*bottom*), and 44. Olympic National Park: 14 (*bottom*), 15 (*bottom*), and 25. Museum of History and Industry: 41, 45, and 56.

SELECTED READINGS

Leissler, Frederick. *Roads and Trails of Olympic National Park.* Seattle and London: University of Washington Press, 1981.

Morgan, Murray. *The Last Wilderness.* Seattle and London: University of Washington Press, 1976.

O'Hara, Pat and Tim McNulty. *Olympic National Park: Where the Mountain Meets the Sea.* Del Mar: Woodlands Press, 1984.

Parratt, Smitty. *God & Goblins: A Field Guide to Place Names of Olympic National Park.* Port Angeles: CP Publications, 1984.

Stewart, Charles. *Wildflowers of the Olympics.* San Francisco: Nature Education Enterprises, 1972.

Tabor, Rowland. *Guide to the Geology of Olympic National Park.* Seattle and London: University of Washington Press, 1975.

Wood, Robert. *Across the Olympic Mountains: The Press Expedition, 1889–90.* Seattle: The Mountaineers, 1967.

Wood, Robert. *Men, Mules and Mountains: Lieutenant O'Neil's Olympic Expeditions:* Seattle: The Mountaineers, 1976.

The paper used in this publication meets the minimum requirements of American National Standard for Information Sciences—Permanence of Paper for Printed Library Materials, ANSI Z39.48-1984. ∞™

Published by Woodlands Press, a division of Robert White & Associates, 853 Camino Del Mar, Del Mar, California 92014

Typography by Boyer & Brass, Inc., San Diego. Lithography by Paragon Press, Salt Lake City.

Library of Congress Cataloging in Publication Data

Steelquist, Robert.
    Olympic National Park and the Olympic Peninsula.

    1. Olympic National Park (Wash.)—Guidebooks. 2. Olympic Peninsula (Wash.)—Description and travel—Guide-books. I. O'Hara, Pat, 1947- . II. McIntyre, Cindy. III. Pacific Northwest National Parks and Forests Association. IV. Title.
F897.O5S77 1985   917.97   85-3223
ISBN 0-917627-06-7